ELBOW SUGAR

DEJA RENE CARR
AKA MAL DEVISA

THE BODILY PRESS
AMHERST, MA

Elbow Sugar

Copyright © 2025 Deja Rene Carr
No part of this book may be used or reproduced in any manner without written permission from the publisher, except in the context of reviews or for educational purposes.
Please address requests for reprint permission to: bodilypress@gmail.com
First Edition, 2025
ISBN: 979-8-9920149-9-0

Cover image:
Jeffrey Lipsky, *Woke up to a Song*, 2025,
Collage and ink on canvas,
16 x 20" (40.6 x 50.8 cm).
All Rights Reserved.
Copyright © 2025 Jeffrey Lipsky
Used by permission of the artist.
facebook.com/JLipArts

Edited by Eliot Cardinaux
Cover Design by Eliot Cardinaux
Layout Design by Eliot Cardinaux
Assistant Layout Design by Alexandra E. Reed
Typset in Cardo, Garamond Premier Pro, DIN 2014
Printed at lulu.com
Published by The Bodily Press
Bodily Press logo designed by Katya Popova

ELBOW SUGAR

Contents

A note on surviving	7
Semicolon	9
Madhouse revisited	10
From Slutwalk to Occupy	11
Do the technicolor Yawn	13
Blue	15
Over Darn that Dream	16
Who's gonna call me gorgeous when the fish have died	18
On Danger's Sun	20
University	23
Thanksgiving	24
All the lovers at half mast	26
Little Wings	31
Snapshot	33
Why I Urge You to Drink Water	34
what she said she's done	38
Whose Hands on the Monument of You	40
Brilliant Mind	42
I imagined spilling boiling coffee on a white shirt in front of you	43
When You Find it Hard to See my Color.	44
As a Human Being	45
Breast	46
Elbow Sugar	47
American Fiction: Thoughts on my life	48

A note on surviving

Clip your nails. You have one. Hour.
I forget, and then watch the dark blue pile up
Underneath these razor blades I hope
You'll remember to love me when I scratch the pigment off
Your face
I'm so sorry
I do not wear this brain a trophy
But it wasn't me
I was
Somehow convinced
It would stop the idle mindedness
Alone now, and much less in the body I mean much more in the body
How am I to know
If you want to survive you'll have to be idle for a moment
Soft for a moment. Learn how to duck and weave, get low, spread out your arms and legs when they
   crowd you
Yes yes,
But only in your head, see?

There are certain things you should know
To do
Mentally— only
In your head.
Yes

Semicolon

Before I leave I throw on a bracelet
2 bracelets
Okay stop berating me, it was 7 bracelets
To make sure they jingle

Not like the other whistles.

Madhouse revisited

I've frequented the madhouse
Drank soup with the endearing hands of slave masters past
And I know only one thing
God listens as if buckled up behind yellow glasses
Of holy water and beer
I joke that when I get up there
They'll hear from me. So I gather the stories of the wicked, drunk, piss drunk, foul, unfortunate, the silly,
  the loose, the pungent lovers with kaftans of broken silk and sit and really listen
So when we get up there, we can borrow the house shoes and smoke cigarettes on the lawn
Oh yes I've frequented the madhouse
My feelings are on sale
And somewhere in hell there is a special place
For the needles stuck into my back and the men
Who get aroused poking holes in my black gold body I keep,
Pictures of my face bloated to feed to the fish along the pond
What can we say about freedom?
Those of us who know the latter side of the hand
Those of us who eat the slop and smile and freak out
What can we say about the sunlight so often called
A privilege. As if you knew god by her name

From Slutwalk to Occupy

The wounded ones
You'd speak for them
Without Question
On the eve of every moment we touch
Hands to show
How brave we were at the Protests
How we celebrate the scathing summer and untouched wrists.
We interrupt the game of spades.

And how to discover you are needed
Be needed. founded on a precedence of non-prejudice
Be shaped all the wrong ways with the right shape of dollar bill lips to speak the unspoken ragged day
   into night

If I were wide eyed enough to say

I love you in a whole chorus voice
Already occupied
Lost on some stranger's form
Already occupied

Some throat with cherries reading open me
Expose me for who I'd be if not for the word…

So the juggernauts walk
And look too much like royalty
Until your eyes have bled
A little bit

Do the technicolor Yawn

Sex is such a pretty thing
Pretty thing, sit down
I promise you can admire yourself
In the armchair of your dreams

Sza sang babylon for the lion in me
Are you hating yourself, do you really hate me?

Bougainvillea brown and split somewhere terrible
Gassed self into self love, bruised apple.

I don't need a manual to kiss my own skin
But she sang it so quietly, my grandmother threw down a pea
And said eat for the times you did the technicolor yawn on purpose

I ate gorgeously and grew pounds heavier
Heavy lips to grab the teeth into submission

And now I'm 28 listening again, to the wrecking night take me in, one vertebrae at a time

Are you hating yourself, do you really hate me?

Blue

I want to find the blue man.
I wonder how he'll sit for tea
Will I begrudgingly grab his finger
And twirl him. Show his lashes and laughter off
Extra
Terrestrial
Blue man
You seek to be understood
And I thought
And I thought skin only came
In such colors as we could count
I know you sought to be holy
Or maybe exist to reminisce about a land with wild grass and taller skies but now you are in my homeland
And I'll treat you well.
Almost like a brother
Stroking the leg of our respective chairs.

Over Darn that Dream

When smoke gets in my eye
I sip my spine straight up, no tonic

Promiscuous heart, she always gathers
At the bosom of things
And they'd never guess how the earth
Spit her out, after many tries to keep her hummin

When smoke gets in my eyes, tinfoil looks like steel bars
Hungry for the hog, i resist and persist with the bird

Sometimes, i bathe for days on end, dripping like library corner
Never once battling the cold, i've grown accustomed to lusting for
Condensation

Unruly, I've been with my kisses, one
On the hand of a rose
One on
The head of a newborn

Save them
For the days only manifesting the color red
Could make you groan ugly at the parlor

Or days when
All you've got are songs for headless beds
Who rock and cradle you

Although you are alone

And you think: who is this phantom man
Making me go mad with delight?

Who's gonna call me gorgeous when the fish have died

I live alone among the rocks
I live alone among the rocks in my room
And now I find it hard to believe in anything but the moon shining through
At that angle that it does

You see
I don't believe in silence and I don't believe in Christmas
I don't believe in sneakers and i don't believe in Vases
I believe in Adeola, my sister, when growing up i knew she was the prettiest person id ever seen
I believe in our eldest, yetunde, face shining like cocoa butter kissed nigeria in languages those two might whisper in my sleep
I believe in folding blankets and offering them to my mother, quietly hoping she chooses the big pillow although I did not say it outloud. Must've forgotten

I live alone amongst the newspapers across the street
I stick my arm out for my neighbor, who crosses the road so fast i couldn't catch her before they swore over her head

I believe in zippers getting caught on Sundays because they are easy to deceive although being easy to deceive doesn't make you worthy of deception.

I believe in clean kitchens and morimoto songs, god's wisdom can never be found on the internet and damn well hard to find over the phone

I belive in changing plans for period pain and weeks in bed crying over art so beautiful i only think of comedy when my mouth opens i believe in so many things

But i live alone amongst the rocks
I live alone amongst the rocks in my room, i devour daylight and eat the splinters in my jeans just to have some room to move around

On Danger's Sun

I rode up a mountain
One tree hill
For devastation
Swept back and forth back and forth
And you didn't get hurt
You didn't get hurt
When I swept you up
For a while
Miracles are inquisitions
Bounty and helium
For the kin of mine to exhale like gospel
I rode up a mountain
One tree hill
With a can on my hip
Nestled close to a man who said I could
And still I didn't

Two sleeping angels sleeping arms length apart
Can you hear this music when it is water gargled between lip and tongue
We broadcasted our love like syllables
Caught on tiger toe
My love is a dove in a cage
Didn't understand why the caged bird didn't sing
And it told me, "look, I just aint the singing kind"
It ruffled me pink
It pulls all my hair
It flies up the stars
Hits the snare in the lip
And calls it Africa resounding for my toes to curl to
Whose one tree, whose hill
Whose backside on fire on the dance floor
I've got qualms with silence dear
With mystery
With questions of whether to and where and why
96 baby spitting forever blue in blue waters
They named me iridescent

They called me his for dinner
They took my bones and scratched the enemy between the brow
So bindi so forgetful, so strong in your absence
Pain and power do not mix
Like   pancake   water   and
Sand   pain   and   power   do
Not mix
But love is forever my drink of choice
Fuck the bourbon, it tried to drown me once
And it was on sale. How could you take
This mountain away
I have no man to climb
No limbs to lose
Only flesh and bone and bravery in my face
To shatter a while, and protrude the darkness with
I scared myself with a picture of a split lipped face
I needed to say
I love you to the laughter.

University

I've angered you for the last time,
I'm writing from a sterile finger on it's last syrupy note
I have nothing to give you but the sides of my stomach
But

I am always excited about being alive
I am not a poet, Black coffee and loafers
But i am a poet of sleepless nights and organic cigarettes
Wading in the government buildings
Government housing

There is something about daylight that be presumptuous
How do you know that I have time to wait until night? To drink water by the tub
To eat the gas station empanada and wish I hadn't
Checking the scale holding nothing but the promise of a clean tomorrow

Someday I will write a play full of arms and legs
They ask me why my music sounds so african
And I tell them
It's the only thing I ever knew how to dance to.

Thanksgiving

My family is a family of thinkers
I am the youngest, Baby Deja with
Her rather fragile smile

Loving is a practice of washing socks
From the distant hallway crashing
Teeth, riots from the kitchen, we laugh
Under stars fluttering Stevie Wonder bright

My brother is a big man. Who forgets me often
Gorgeous as they come.
How do I let him know
That my heart is golden, and fades not in the darkness
Of an untamed state. I eat my tea alone today…2 lectures in

My sisters have dreams of their own, and do not know
That i count the syllables in their names to teach to my children
For when they come they shall know there once were two women
With your mother's arms, who dreamt their way to freedom

My mother is a jokester. She feels the past and the future
And puts bandages on the world where it's left itself in a bind
But sometimes forgets her own poultice and the wound of being Black
And bold in America, and woman in a time where stoic
Hearts guard the money in a white mans box

Loving is a practice of washing bras, praying for a one-day balcony
Splitting already-split peas at the table, and cursing the rain
When all you wanted to do
Was see your kin unscathed by it all

And I am alone today. 2 lectures in
Wondering when my neighbor might finish cooking
A stranger in a stranger home, no longer a stranger to me
With five fingers ready for a warm book and a tv remote
2 lectures in and I can't count how many times
I've tried to wish away a holiday for reasons others may deem
So selfish

All the lovers at half mast

All the lovers at half mast
I bruised my hip carrying lemons on my arm
Pretending i was a waitress
A job I could never keep because I forget too much.

And all the women in the world are circling tongue and water
Inviting hilarity in, for a righteous god to try on.

Where is she? The Sun

I didn't hit him when he stared
I didn't dip the seams of my dress in berry juice
Just to be surveilled
I've walked through storms in the snow

I love you when you are not missing in plain site
I love you when you are mischievous alone in your skin
Not my hand, which i fondle flowers with i'd be remiss
If i didn't kiss you once upon the lips

You love me for the flock of lightning that I am
But I promise you this

I will not wander in my head and say
I, I, I, all alone.

But perfection comes to these legs when left unhugged
And I cannot stand to open them, not anymore, not yet

For adulting ears to listen to vocals swimming pearly white
Cough coughing it up break break up tobacco on the hinds of a gospel layer

I love you when you are yours first, please do not be afraid to walk into yourself
I love you even though you are afraid to be alone and love my company

I think we are healthy enough to part like birds becoming anew
Mic check i said i think we are healthy enough to park like birds becoming clouds

Brown edges on these feathers, they got dipped in tar, chipped like teeth, dazzled down, fought to earn,
Edges blue, slivers of dawn, returning like the alabama breeze to bite down

And i have no jaw strong like my ancestors
They bring the sides to every thought, they bring me

Darling yooooooooooou send me
You send me
Darling you send me

So uncage me for the night time
For the day bringing soot into vein

Because everybody wants to be yours
But it takes a woman to think on her own

Alone in her head
Fat arms in a white bed

We mismatch, we mismatched
I ask and then I axe and then i'm here

Then i'm here,
To regain the loose match I've found for future fires
In my brain

My loose intelligent back snapping at every orifice

No hell below for my sin of loving too correctly

I've bit 81 bullets in my life
And never chipped my navel on them

I forget the now, and remember 3 seconds from now
I know how we get down, again.

The   radio   on
Mute the children
Sleep   the   parents
Sleep
And the youngings go wild

The   radio   on
Mute the children
Sleep   the   parents
Sleep
And we pout our fists at the shadows

Aching like the canvas before black
We march on,

When my father calls me, he says he aiight in patois
Before hanging up.

When i call my father i secretly thank him
For leaving me alone.

So try and do the same
I need your mind like i need blood
But your body i can do without

Try and do the same
I Love you like i love white rice
But a clogged heart can't dance to your condiment beat
Beauty in black

I love you like i love white rice but candy them yams
For a different sistah.

Little Wings

But I can sing, little wings
In the corridor and try and find you
Wrapped around the table like a saucer
Hearing the flutter of breaths

Bare pencil shavings on the floor
"But I can sing little wings"
And try and find you
Perfumed in the chaos of seattle
Diseased in the beauty of new york
Lipstick stains on the collar of your red coat
We can sing

And now the smoke has fallen from my nose bone
And I cannot sing. But I can grow strawberries on the window
Until i get enough from the wilderness
Underground native

Don't be confused when you are 21
By the glossed up pack on your boyfriends floor
Eat grapes. Write songs. And fight the crime of being
Don't announce to the dorm room who they are in the context of things
While writing on a marijuana cloud

And when you quit
Quit for good.

Snapshot

Lukewarm camera
Focus, not the camera
It'self but the image
If i were talking about the camera itself
It would be redundant
But I am not
I promise i'm not
Are you laughing at my head or my feet
I smell a poem under the bed

Why I Urge You to Drink Water
For Nikki Carr

When I think of a face, sullen in the sun
Or freezing in the warmth of an eastern day
And also think, of someone who i'd want to know
No pain

Know no pain
No jagged edge in life or protruding doubt in the rain

I think of you.
I've always thought it was strange to call a person home
Maybe due to the mobile nature of people and how they
Move
Through spaces in your life, through furrowed and borrowed time
I've never been afraid of being alone. I Welcome the darkness,
It's kin.

But to move around you. Know our legs a trophy, wicked as the night.
To inherit the brightness of a smile is to know
Home spins you and makes you walk. Because you laugh when you fall

I haven't fallen in years.
I've learned to use these legs.
You don't drink
But I couldn't wrestle a soda from you
And i urge you to drink a half cup of
Water for every can.

Because we gamble with the wind by just being human
And sometimes, I want to know and be sure
Your cells are watered
Like the dew on a freshly baked sidewalk
Someone tripped. We might laugh
We might not.

::

I've never worn true religion jeans
I've never been to fashion week
I've never sipped wine in the moonlight begging for a kiss

However the song goes it is not mine
And not mine at all
But I have walked along the beach in the puffy wind
And asked for things to be mine to keep
By the refrigerator, a picture made of wood and glass
And gasped at the news in my hand me downs
Does that make me an American
Be it the only title I didn't ask for
The American poet, always late never smitten
Or riding in the fast lane with a driver whose last name rolls off the tongue
Spiced rum and the chatter of good folk
To tell the youth not to follow in my footsteps
America casts a glaze on the comings and goings of it all
The rituals we create in the night with two naked feet and a candle
Does that alternate your ears to the sound
Of a Poet with no little army and a basket of roses and rocks to give
And to keep
A crystal to sell on eBay
A body that needs constant guarding as if it meant something to somebody.
As if I meant something to somebody brave.
I do.

And although I've never worn true religion jeans
Never laughed at the fashion house
I wear my flares
Eat my seeds
And belong to someone
A life to be lived in adjacency to some afternoon black
Woman with shoulders made of rubies
And home in her smile that always made me think
You look like someone to love

what she said she's done

i must have licked the shoulder
of a sober poet
why else
would there be daisies lifting up
my heels
why else
would there be no alarm
to live by no false dawn
and croak the songs
of false idols
well i don't know
your fathers name
or where you came from
but come again
come at dawn with ample time to swear to
me i am still as beautiful
as when i was nineteen
still as hungry and menacing
still

the lemon balm broken on your fingertips
the buzzing toe and dance for silver
still as hungry and menacing
still bound for glory

Whose Hands on the Monument of You

Massive Massive night
I took a star under the pit of my arm
And hoped it would sway my hips
Like the guiding of a tusk in motherland
How between the eyes forged a path

And if tonight I am let go
From the face of this earth
I hope my dad moonwalks in the bronx

A Jamaican man with a soft voice and
Hard hands
Hands that say I had to
Work a day or two to build
You

Calluses run in my family
My father builds sheet rock
At 60.

Skinny as a bird with strong lungs

He is God's example of the distant reggae song in our heads
Playing over and over
And sometimes, I think of him

Leaning over me to tell me
You out of anyone can name man what they are

You out of anyone knows
The truth

Brilliant mind

I   want   that   flower   in   your
Hand I'm watching a movie called stutz with Jonah Hill and his therapist
Forgetting in the ether that my therapist laughs and smiles and I stare
Lifeless because I wish I could hold her hand
In a friendly way

She asked me how it felt to have a white therapist
And I lie
I say, "you know, I really don't mind it. I like it"
And I felt small Deja, whose hands were stuck on her hips
And whose words pierced and cut until it told you how she felt…
I felt her roll her eyes like dice in craps type crap

I imagined spilling boiling coffee on a white shirt in front of you

I'd erupt into laughter
The way girls in love do
So beauty
Reminding the populous I'm okay
But better than okay
Really
And with a brush of dawn
We walk a caress' love letter down a street   in Paris
But some Paris not on Earth
The trees are located in a state somewhere
Rugged with sagged branches and malted chocolate thanking sunrise and sunshine
And all things that glow
In the left wings backstage
Because in life
There will always be beautiful brown boys who run through new dance moves like manuscripts all early on
The beat like a new
And distinct
Detroit
Rapper thank
U

When You Find it Hard to See my Color.

there shouldn't be a manual. at first,
i toyed with the assumption that i had to assimilate
but most of me kindly
notices
appreciates
how standing out, is a beacon of blue cool light in a sepia room
however beautiful, struggling to know its veins.
i know, that i can't listen to strawberry by paul baribeau without feeling in love
with a boy i do not know who is different from the boys who have told me there was nothing between us,
    and then smiled at the moon as if i were up there
despite tomorrow and yesterday, and full fledged misery on the arm of the sofa
my hair cleansed the clean from the room

no manual, no fist no yearning
and i remember the pugnacious words of my grandmother
leaning over my bath
and keep them a secret.

As a human being

Where am i going to find
A woman like me
To share recipes
Of lemon water

Ginger under the arm
To stop the men from running
Peace to the women with bones of nectar
Who never run from the mirror

At any time
Of day

Breast

Sweetness swinging low
You asked for this country with your chin
I would bend over backwards to explain that
No one is coming to take your lighter from
You nor your beautifully sitting cigarette

I want you to love your sisters
But maybe I am ignorant in thinking
You are one of them

I heard through the grapevine that you don't like those with two names
That you hate the way no curves turns into lampshade silhouette

I asked for this country with all of these lamps in motion
With breasts and beard, black and blue, beaten face, sun drenched lips, beauty mark drawn on

Elbow sugar

I want a kiss
From a man who takes me so seriously
The birds fly in formation with me in mind
Elbow sugar,
In flight or in stillness we arrive at midnight: a chords collision,
Lovely spoonful of sand for the foot and hand

American Fiction: Thoughts on my life

Will they still put me in the ocean
If i cannot swim
Will they carry my ashes, laden with my voice across the caribbean back home
Somewhere in a land where the fists speak volumes of poetry never written down
Will the water feel like salt on exited spirit wounding the throat, caressing the back

Maybe they'll float a casket on the lake
Light it afire
A type of heroes cremation

I find that thinking about death

Prepares me for life, a snap of the finger
Up and at em
Through the ring and glistening snow

I am sitting in my new apartment
Fixated on bukowski and the hundreds of books that surround me
Nothing could beat

Coming home
Alive and fat
Stretched out like a sea of limbs
But breathing

Hope to never catch you with your head down
In my rear view

Acknowledgments

Thank you to Nikki Carr and Paul Lewis, my very different but wonderful parents. Haniyf, Ade, Yeye and all of my nieces and nephews. To all of my English teachers, including Jamison Isler, y'all the real mvps.

Thank you to the valley and all of the musicians who raised and mentored me. To Who'da, to Masla, to those who housed and fed me.

Thank you to PVPA and IMA. June Millington and Ann Hackler, and thank you to all of you who read my work and make it possible for me to feel like it makes a difference in people's lives.

Thank you to Ruvi Ender, my best friend, for encouraging me to keep making art and for loving the product of my very chaotic brain and to Emily Moran my longtime best friend from Hampshire for being the sweetest person in the world and holding on to me even when I didn't want to be wanted.

Thank you to the Bodily Press.

And to everyone I've met along the way, thank you.
You're in my heart.

About the Author

DEJA RENE (pronounced Rheen) CARR is a 28 year old Poet, Artist, Musician, Conceptual Artist, Comedian born in Manhattan NY, now residing in Amherst Mass. She spent her first two collegiate years at Hampshire College and is now completing her BA in English at Umass Amherst. Her art is wide-reaching, at times chaotic, funny yet arresting, and beautifully rooted in the Black experience of the fringe-space. She lives by the phrase: The personal is political, and never shys to show us the underbelly of the American Psyche she was raised and steeped in. "So much of what I do is in an attempt to write about love, and then I realize, maybe there are prerequisites to knowing love. It exists all along, yes, but to know it as a whole on a systemic level, there might be some ideas to wade through first." Deja Carr is also Mal Devisa, her main artistic project that weaves story telling, beats of various genres, and previously performance art with her unmistakable raw voice. She loves poetry and poets an incredible amount and wants to thank The Bodily Press for being a wonderful outlet for her new work.

The Bodily Press
bodilypress.bandcamp.com
www.bodilypress.com
@thebodilypress